Resume

The Definitive Guide on Writing a Professional Resume to Land You Your Dream Job

David Barron

Golden Road Publishing

Table of Contents

Introduction: Opening New and Exciting Opportunities

Creating an interesting, informative, and polished resume is the key that unlocks the doors of opportunity in today's demanding workplace. The challenges employers face when sifting through the hundreds of resumes from hopeful candidates makes this process tedious and quite unrewarding for them. Many companies apply a screening process that uses keyword searches and specific formatting criteria to pre-qualify candidates. If you don't know how to play the game, your resume will never win you an interview.

The following chapters will discuss how to create an incredible resume that will get you the job you've always dreamed of having. You'll learn what to include in your resume, the type of resume that best suits your purpose, and how to make it a marketing tool that sells you to your prospective employer in the best possible light. After reading *Resume: The Definitive Guide on Writing a Professional Resume to Land You Your Dream Job*, you'll be able to write and design a resume that will capture the interest of any prospective employer and open the door to greater heights of achievement on your career path.

Chapter 1: It's All About Getting the Interview

After spending an hour creating your resume, you're thinking you can just randomly post it on multiple job sites and watch the offers roll in, right? If that's all it took to find your dream job, there would be so many qualified candidates in front of you, that you'd never have the opportunity to interview with your prospective employer. That's what a professional resume is all about—getting the interview.

Some candidates consider the resume a tool used to impress the hiring manager with their creative design and a long list of experience and education. If you're one such candidate, most likely your previous efforts have been rewarded with few responses and even fewer interviews. In fact, there's a good chance your resume never even passed the preliminary screening process.

Key words? Screening process? If you think these terms only apply to those looking for technological positions, think again. The resumes that get results in today's job market are those that create interest and relate to the prospective employer's specific needs. If not, they won't make it through the first cut by the Applicant Tracking System (ATS).

What's an Applicant Tracking System (ATS)?

ATS is software that helps managers match the position's job description with the candidate's skills and experiences. The software uses phrases, themes, and keywords that align with the posted job description to weed through the hundreds, or thousands, of resumes to find what they consider to be the best-qualified applicants. Unfortunately, your skills and experience could be far superior to those who make the cut, but because you failed to format your resume properly, you didn't make it past the circular file.

If you have practiced the "one-size-fits-all" approach to resume writing, it's time for you to change your mindset. One carefully crafted, specific resume is more effective than 100 general resumes randomly submitted to companies in hopes of getting an interview. Since 75 percent of larger companies use ATS, and 60 percent of the mid-sized ones do as well, it is to your benefit to learn how to structure your resume first to pass the Applicant Tracking System.

Using Key Words to Pass Through ATS

ATS uses its software to identify key words in your resume. These key words come from the job posting itself. For example, if the job description states the ideal candidate will have a proven track record in sales, have excellent communication skills, and be a self-starter, then your resume should address all these points using some key words to describe the skills you have that match these specific requirements. The words you'll want to use to describe your skills should match those that would give evidence to the keywords or terms in the resume. So, let's examine the key points from the job description and then list some descriptive words that would be used by a candidate that had these skills.

Key Words from Posting

Sales, Communications, Self-Starter

Descriptive Words

For Sales: Marketing, Promoting, Persuading

For Communications: Writing, Speaking, Listening, Developing

For Self-Starter: Initiating, Leading, Managing, Directing

Notice that all the descriptive words are action verbs. These words not only describe what an excellent salesperson, communicator, and self-starter would do, but they also keep the reviewer's interest because they carry the action. Of course, you should only include the descriptive words that accurately represent you. If you do not know how to market or promote, then you would want to use words that are a better match for your skills. For example, if you wanted to speak of your sales skills, but you feel you are better selling by compromise or getting others to come to an agreement, then use those words. If the words that describe your communications skills lean more toward writing than speaking, then use examples with the words to describe writing in the content.

As you progress through the book, you'll learn where and how to use these words in your resume. It's always a good idea to think like an employer. Create a compelling resume that shows managers how your skills can benefit them. Don't use the words "I," "me," or "my," when you're describing your unique skills and achievements.

Using Proper Formatting to Pass Through ATS

Formatting types, styles, and selection will be discussed in another chapter. The format we are talking about here is referring to the structure that will enable you to make it through ATS. The following are five formatting tips to help you get your resume to the hiring manager.

1.   Avoid using a resume template or text boxes, even when submitting your resume online. When submitting resumes online, create a text-only version.

2.   Use standard fonts like Georgia, Cambria, Helvetica, or Times New Roman. Use black

ink, and avoid colored graphics or shading. If you want to dress up your resume, do so with the one you give to the prospective employer in person to avoid being tripped up going through ATS. Submit your resume as a .pdf file, and save your creative versions for later. A good rule of thumb for font sizes is 14-16 point for your name and 10-12 point for the body of your resume.

3. Margins should be approximately one inch on all sides, top, and bottom.

4. Use a Microsoft Word document; avoid creating your resume in Publisher or another designer program that might not be as convenient to open, or ATS will reject that.

5. Don't fold your resume. If it is more than one page, and you want to avoid this when possible, label the second page with a header that includes your name, contact information, and page number.

Have you ever watched a commercial on television and genuinely liked the commercial but later couldn't have told anyone what product or service was being advertised? Thousands of dollars wasted on an entertaining or interesting commercial that promotes the unknown. Unfortunately, this happens to resumes all the time. The candidate might be well-suited to the posted position, and the resume looks great, so what could go wrong?

Candidates often forget to clearly state their purpose, the position, and the direct benefits of hiring them. Their resume looks great, but it's not clear to the prospective employer what position is being applied for, and what benefits they would receive if they were to hire this person. Sure, it's pleasing to the eye, and that says something about you, but it doesn't inspire the employer to pick up the phone and call you in for an interview.

What Else Should Your Resume Do?

Once you've decided what keywords or phrases to use, and how to match your skills with the job posting, you'll also need to deliver information like education, experience, and some basic facts. Where you put this information, and the importance you give it, will depend on the position, your core strengths, and skills, and the style of resume you choose to present that will place you in the best light.

You'll notice there is no mention of putting references on your resume. Yesterday's resume format used to include a list of references, or just a statement at the bottom of the page that read *"references available upon request."* In today's job market, it is understood that you will supply those at the interview, so there is no need to add that statement. Once you have included all the relevant skills and achievements and basic facts, you'll probably be pushing that bottom line and need the room to fit everything onto one page.

Story at a Glance

John Lees, author of the book *Knockout CV* and professional career strategist, reinforced the fact that there's not much time to make a good first impression. He states, "The first 15-20 words of your resume are critically important because that's how long you usually have a hiring manager's attention." It can be quite time consuming for busy managers to sift through hundreds of resumes in hopes of finding a handful of qualified applicants. The more responsibilities they must set aside to perform the hiring task, the more stressed they become in the process.

A clear, well-written and formatted resume will tell your story at a glance. Managers should be able to give your resume a quick glance and determine several important aspects of your personality and working career. Here are some of the things they should know within 20 seconds:

- The position for which you are applying

- Your qualifications will exceed their expectations

- Your attention to detail will prove beneficial in the position

- You are an excellent communicator

- You understand their needs and wants

- You have concrete achievements that demonstrate your stated skills and knowledge

- You have worked in related fields or jobs with similar demands

- You are an organized person

- You are a leader who takes initiative

If you have formatted and written your resume well, hiring managers will glean all this information in a glance, and they will appreciate your efforts to make their job easier. If you have not done a good job with your resume, they will also learn that quickly as well. At just a glance, you can give the prospective employer a reason to place your resume in the "no interview" pile. Some of those reasons can be caused by the following:

- Spelling or grammatical errors

- Poor organization

- No focus or clearly-stated objective or summary

- Gaps in your job history

- Embellished lists of skills and qualifications

- No specific achievements

- The resume is too long

- You simply aren't qualified for the position

Good or bad, your resume sends a message about you; make sure that message represents you in a positive light. If you expect the hiring manager to spend their valuable time interviewing you, be willing to put your valuable time into creating a dynamic, interesting, and informative resume. Do all that you can to convince managers that they would be missing out on an incredible employee if they passed up the opportunity to interview you. Your resume is like a movie trailer; it should give the reader a preview of what's to come and create anticipation to meet you in person.

In Preparation of Your Resume

First, make up your mind that you're not going to complete your resume in an hour and then go do something else that's more interesting. Get comfortable, gather your information, and plan to spend some time creating a resume that will leave prospective employers wanting more. A word of caution for those of you who are considering using a professional resume writer to do the work for you. That may work for you "one-size-fits-all" submitters, but if you buy into the fact that tailoring your resume for each employer gives you the upper hand, you'll run up quite a tab using the service.

The average cost of having a professional design a resume for you is approximately $250-$600 each. Think about it—do you want to shell out $250 for every resume you send? By the time you get the resume completed, there's a good chance the position you wanted will be filled. Even if you are thinking that you could slightly change your professionally-written resume for every position for which you wish to apply, think again.

To tailor your resume, you would need to modify the objective or summary and reorder and re-emphasize your stated achievements, perhaps even change the formatting to organize the relevant information differently depending on the employer's stated needs. You simply cannot make one or two changes to a resume and expect positive results. Why not save yourself the money and time, keep reading, and learn to create your own resume? After all, who is more qualified to tell your story than you?

The most important thing when writing your resume is to be honest about your skills. Don't embellish—not even a little. When you view the job posting and see something that you are not qualified to do, don't try to fake it 'til you make it; the prospective employer can spot that a mile away. Think of the employer's requirements as a wish list. In a perfect world, a candidate with all those skills would be their wish. However, in the real world, most employers understand that they are not going to find the perfect person to fill the position.

Hiring managers don't expect you to know everything, so stop pretending like you do. Emphasize your strengths, and don't apologize for your weaknesses. Just show them through your stated skills that you're the type of person who takes the initiative to learn new skills. A study done by Career Builders in August of 2014 surveyed 2,000 hiring managers. They said that 57 percent of the lies they catch on resumes were because candidates embellished their skills set.

It's always a better practice to be straight forward. Remember, the primary purpose of your resume is to get you the interview. The truth is, most candidates that are invited for an interview may not be the most qualified, but they are the most interesting and the ones that have a professional-looking resume.

Chapter 2: Formatting & Fonts

Prospective employers see a variety of resume types and styles, and some resumes that have no format or particular style. Contrary to what some "maverick" resume designers may think, there are only three major types of resumes that are widely considered acceptable. They are the chronological, the functional, and the combination resumes. Let's examine them further and see what type of resume is the best fit for the kind of position you are applying for.

The Chronological Resume

The chronological resume is the most commonly used and the most traditional of the three types. The focus of this type of resume is one's job experience, and because of this, it is most effective when you are applying for a job in the same profession or field, or at least a job that has similar tasks. Many in law or academia use this type of resume. It is by far the most recognized of the resume types, appealing to those more traditional or conservative types of hiring managers.

It is sometimes referred to as the "reverse chronological resume" because your job experiences are listed from your current job or latest position backward. One mistake many candidates make when using this type of resume is that they try to list too many jobs. You don't need to go back to your first job out of high school. If you want to keep your resume to one page, list your last company and then go back no more than ten years.

The disadvantage to using a chronological resume is that it is difficult to differentiate yourself from the hundreds of others because of the challenges of highlighting your achievements. If you want to stand out in the crowd, and the company you are applying to is not ultra conservative, then you may want to use a combination format. You'll see a sample of that one later. The advantages of using this format are that it is perhaps the easiest and clearest to glean information from, and the strongest format to get you through the ATS screening system.

Since the chronological resume emphasizes job experience, it is definitely not the type to use if you are short on experience or if you have time gaps between jobs. Later in the book, you'll learn about others that are more effective for those situations. This is a sample of the chronological resume, and its details will be examined in another chapter.

Sample Chronological Resume

John Doe

111 W. Latham St.
        480-880-9090
Tempe, AZ 00401
       jdoe@gmail.com

OBJECTIVE:
   Senior marketing position with a publishing company that values expertise in multimedia production and strategic website development.

EDUCATION:
   Bachelor of Arts, Arizona State University, Tempe, AZ
Major: Marketing/Communications   GPA 3.90/4.00
Graduated Summa Cum Laude

WORK HISTORY:
2008-Present

DSS Enterprises, Phoenix, AZ
Marketing Director
- Developed ad tracking system that increased sales revenue from $3.1 million to $9 million over a 24-month period
- Persuaded Arizona's top 10 corporate executives to utilize our website design services, resulting in a $2.4 million increase over a five-years period
- Recruited a 12-member design team specializing in business-to-business multimedia production, decreasing outsourced cost

	by $600,000 over a 12-month period
1997-2008	**Webmasters, Tempe, AZ** *Senior Designer*

1997-2008   **Webmasters, Tempe, AZ**
Senior Designer

- Coordinated production of a team of six website designers and two multimedia specialists, presiding over five print and two online publications with a 30-day turn-around
- Negotiated 18 client agreements that saved $200,000 over a five-year period
- Designed Arizona's website of the year for 2006

SPECIAL SKILLS: Proficient in Adobe Illustrator and Photoshop, QuarkXpress, Wix, Weebly, Squarespace

ACTIVITIES: Member of Arizona Cyber Club for Website Designers
Trainer for World Championship Tennis Association

The Functional Resume

Instead of highlighting previous job experiences, the functional resume emphasizes relevant accomplishments and skills. This type of resume is an excellent choice for those who may have some employment gaps or who are changing career paths. The functional resume allows you the freedom to lift portions of several of your jobs to demonstrate to your employer that you have the skills for a particular position.

If you are returning to the workplace after having had several years working from home or perhaps have been away in the service, the functional resume will help you smooth over those work disconnections. If questioned in your interview, you can explain those situations away. Keep in mind, the objective of your resume is to get you the interview.

The advantage to using the functional resume is that it enables the hiring manager to quickly determine that your skills and achievements will be a good fit for the position. The downside, though, is that your previous company and the duties you had with that company are not as clear. If your former employer is more impressive than your current skill set, then you'll want to use the chronological resume.

As you begin developing the functional resume, describing your skills and the benefits they bring to the table will be important. Make sure you place your skills and achievements in the top half of your resume. If the hiring manager is giving your resume a 20-second scan, you will want him or her to see your skills and achievements right away. Your work history and education can go in the bottom half of the resume.

Reading through the functional resume, notice the formatting and category differences as well. The functional resume has several sections rather than one large area. The categories are also placed in reverse with the skills and qualifications at the top and education at the bottom.

Another important note on both the chronological and functional resumes are that the year you graduated has no date. If your GPA wasn't top notch, there is also no need to list it on your resume. You do want to put dates on your job history, but if you decide to do so for your education, it might reveal your age, which for some could be a problem.

Of the three types of resumes, this is probably the least used. Instead of a functional resume, many candidates decide to use the combination resume. We'll look at that one a little later.

Sample Functional Resume
JOHN DOE
111 W. Latham St.
Tempe, Arizona 00401
cell: 602-222-2232 • home: 480-880-9090
• jdoe@gmail.com

OBJECTIVE: Position as a Secondary School Teacher with district that will utilize core teaching abilities
to create a stimulating learning environment to help young adults achieve their potential

QUALIFICATIONS:

- Over 20 years experience teaching 9th, 10th, and 11th grade English and Creative Writing
- Bachelor's Degree from Arizona State University—Graduated Summa Cum Laude
- Curriculum developer for 9th, 10th, and 11th grade English Courses
- Head of English Department for five years
- Mastery learning and core skills outcome-based teaching

RELEVANT SKILLS:

- Developed curriculum for pilot American Literature/American History course, resulting in national presentations and adoptions of program in high schools across the country
- Acted as Department Chair for staff of 16 teachers for a period of five years
- Awarded Arizona Teacher of the Year in 2015

- Wrote outcome-based lesson plans for Glendale Union High School District over a period of nine years, which were distributed to all English teachers throughout state
- Organized benchmarks for grant proposal that resulted in A+ rating for Apollo High School

WORK HISTORY:

Apollo High School   Glendale, AZ
                              1994-Present
   English Teacher/Department Head

Princeton High School   Cincinnati, OH
                              1987-1994
   English Teacher

VOLUNTEER EXPERIENCE:

PTA Coordinator for Apollo High School   Glendale, AZ
                              2014-2016

EDUCATION and TRAINING

Arizona State University   Tempe, AZ

   Secondary Education/English

The Combination Resume

The combination resume does exactly what it says—it combines elements of both the chronological and functional resumes. It begins with a qualifications and achievements section and then the second half contains the chronology of previous jobs. The advantage to this type of resume is that the candidate takes advantage of the positives of both types, emphasizing skills and achievements while also providing valuable information about previous jobs and experience that are relevant to this position. The disadvantage is that these kinds of resumes tend to be longer, and they can also be repetitious.

More and more highly specialized professionals are leaning toward the combination resume, realizing that the information and skills to be included will extend past one page anyway. If you have a lot of work experience, an extensive education, and a wide range of related skills, it's acceptable to extend your resume beyond the first page. However, continue to be concise with your words, omitting the fluff that tends to sound pretentious.

The candidates who need to use this type of resume often have impressive references. They often include several of those references at the end of their resume, especially if the names are well-known in the industry. Many candidates have had doors opened to them because of who they knew as well as what they knew. If it makes your resume more powerful, don't be afraid to name drop.

While it's important not to embellish your skills, that doesn't mean you can't toot your own horn. If you do possess a unique skill or have achieved award-winning status in your industry, by all means—shout it out. If you have volunteered for an exciting project or world-renown cause, let your hiring manager know about it by emphasizing it in your resume. It's surprising how many people have been given opportunities because they were a high-ranking military, naval officer or because they interned under a doctor or lawyer with celebrity status.

A word of caution is warranted here. When touting your achievements or awards, write them in such a way as to sound honored and proud to have been involved with that person or project. Be careful you don't come off sounding like a braggart.

The following combination resume will demonstrate how to create a story-at-a-glance as well as provide information that is necessary to show you are qualified for the position.

Sample Combination Resume

JANE DOE

111 W. Latham St.
Tempe, Arizona 85041
Home: 480-880-9090
Cell: 602-222-2232
Email: jdoe@gmail.com

OBJECTIVE: Seeking creative writing opportunity with responsibilities to include researching, writing, program development, and editing.

QUALIFICATIONS: Published 22 books and hundreds of national magazine articles as director of Published & Professional Ghost Writers Association for the past 20 years. I am proficient in:

Research & Development
               Production
EBook Writing & Design
               Textual Organization
Interviewing
               Time Management

ACHIEVEMENTS: <u>Director of Published & Professional Ghost Writers</u>. Researched and ghost wrote both fiction and non-fiction books. Currently, have books in bookstores and Amazon. Wrote and developed speaking programs for national sales trainers. Ghost wrote hundreds of articles for national publications.

Managing Editor for Western Pacific Airlines In-flight Magazine—*Skyview*. Researched destination cities and stimulated city leadership participation in the in-flight magazine.

Training Coordinator, Publisher & Contributing Writer— *Broker/Agent Magazine*. Opened the largest Broker/Agent trade magazine in the history of the company. Trained other national publishers and contributed hundreds of articles in dozens of city editions across the country.

EXPERIENCE: PUBLISHED & PROFESSIONAL GHOST WRITERS   1990-Present Director/Writer & Program Developer

THE WEST GROUP

2000-2010 Director of Program Development

APOLLO HIGH SCHOOL

1987-1992 High School English Teacher

EDUCATION: Arizona State University

1987 Graduated with 3.8 GPA/Summa Cum Laude

REFERENCES: (add on second page)

Choosing the Right Font

To illustrate the difference between easy-to-read fonts and those that make the text look busy and cluttered, look at the three different font styles and let your eyes rest on the text for no longer than 20 seconds:

Now is the time for all good men to come to the aid of their country. Now is the time for all good men to come to the aid of their country. Now is the time for all good men to come to the aid of their country.

Now is the time for all good men to come to the aid of their country. Now is the time for all good men to come to the aid of their country. Now is the time for all good men to come to the aid of their country.

Now is the time for all good men to come to the aid of their country. Now is the time for all good men to come to the aid of their country. Now is the time for all good men to come to the aid of their country.

Although it's difficult to tell, all three of the above fonts are the same size. However, the clarity and ease at which one can read the print are significantly impacted by the font style. Font choice should not be based on the letter artistry, but rather on the legibility of the letters. It's not just about the size of the font, but also the spacing between letters and words. Even the first font, which is called Arial, is more compact and a bit harder to read than Georgia, which is the font used in the text for this book (these words you're reading right now).

Also, avoid using title lettering, even if it's black ink. Title lettering might be cause for your resume to fail the ATS screening. The following fonts are ones that are clear, and usually, don't create any red flags for ATS:

- Georgia
- Helvetica
- Arial
- Cambria
- Garamond
- Times New Roman

Avoid using several different fonts on your resume; it can look confusing and unorganized if you change fonts. Some like to change fonts for the titles. If you want to create uniformity and consistency, use only one font. Also, resist the temptation to bold and italicize words or phrases. You can bold your name and the resume categories, but don't bold skills and qualifications or awards. Too much bold and italics looks unprofessional. Let your skills and qualifications speak for themselves.

By now you should have an idea of what type of resume you plan on using: chronological, functional, or combination. You should also have settled on a proper font that is clear and pleasing to the reader, and that shows professionalism and style. All these elements of the resume are more for aesthetic value than the development and verbiage, which is the subject of a later chapter.

Chapter 3: From the Employer's Perspective

There are a few disturbing truths that job seekers must face, and that is that as eager and prepared as you are in your job-seeking endeavors, prospective employers don't feel the same excitement and anticipation. It's a crazy job market, and most people are expected to do the job of two or three—including the hiring manager who is reviewing your resume. With the added time it takes to recruit, interview, and hire a new employee, their already tight schedules are overloaded with the burden of going through stacks of resumes, some so absurd as to be laughable.

Smaller companies that do not use an ATS system are forced to review candidates who either don't qualify for the position or ones who are using this job as a stop-gap until something else better comes along. Sadly, they also review resumes from people who genuinely would be great for the company but didn't put together a reputable resume, so their efforts are in vain.

It's not that employers are cold and callous when it comes to reviewing your resume; their lack of interest and perceived boredom comes from hours of resume reviewing with no viable candidates to show for it. If you are one of the lucky ones and happen to make the first cut past the ATS to the employer's desk, now you've got to make sure your resume 'wows' the hiring manager.

Creating a resume that wows doesn't mean you need to use bright pink paper and decorate your resume with graphic art. Quite the opposite! Put yourself in the place of the employer, and you'll soon see what they are looking for in your resume. There is no magic formula, no guaranteed winning resume. You and your skills are unique, and your resume should reflect that fact. It should tell your individual story and be written and designed for that one particular job posting.

To make your resume represent you, not only do you have to provide information about your qualifications, skills, and past experiences, but you also need to show your soft skills. Let's break down what is meant by soft skills.

How Do You Sell Your Soft Skills?

How can you sell your soft skills if you don't even know what they are, right? Well, soft skills are those things about you that make it easy for others to work with you. For example, you'll want the hiring manager to know that you can work well on a team, that you are responsible and reliable, that you can take the initiative and be a leader, and that you can identify and solve problems.

While many of these soft skills can be shared in a cover letter, the fact is that prospective employers never read most of the candidates' cover letters. Employers have enough on their hands just to get through the stack of resumes; there is precious little time left over for cover letters. For this reason, it's a good idea to include everything you want the manager to see within the resume. So, how do you show the soft skills? Easy! You display your soft skills by the words you use in your resume.

The words you use will show strength, character, and all the things that drive and inspire you. Look at the list of words below that will let an employer know about your soft skills.

Words That Show Responsibility

Dependable	Responsible	Committed
Motivated	Dedicated	Loyal
Determined	Attentive	Diligent
Trustworthy	Disciplined	Reliable

Words That Show You Are a Team Player

Collaborate	Volunteer	Contribute
Participate	Represent	Coach
Facilitate	Mediate	Resolve
Clarify	Support	Demonstrate

Words That Show You Are Organized

Arrange	Implement	Define
Maintain	Catalog	Organize
Schedule	Distribute	Outline
Prepare	Report	Order

Words That Show You Have a Positive Attitude

Sensitive	Understanding	Enthusiastic
Adaptable	Consistent	Energetic
Passionate	Receptive	Willing
Open-minded	Positive	Empathetic

Word That Show You Are Creative

Design	Illustrate	Market
Promote	Plan	Compose
Establish	Develop	Originate
Initiate	Create	Introduce

These are words you can use in your resume that reveal your soft skills—more of your character and attitude. They differ from the words you use to describe your more concrete skills, such as the following.

Words That Describe You as a Leader

Delegate	Mediate	Eliminate
Attain	Generate	Lead
Review	Resolve	Improve
Incorporate	Direct	Assign

Words That Describe Your Technical Skills

Compute	Repair	Maintain
Operate	Solve	Calculate
Assemble	Upgrade	Build
Overhaul	Troubleshoot	Train

Think of your resume as a self-brand you are creating to promote yourself with words. The employer cannot see you, so you must create an image with your words. For maximum results, the image you create should match the image the employer has in mind for his or her candidate of choice. The National Association of Colleges and Employers (NACE) ranked the top ten attributes employers look for on a candidate's resume as follows:

1. Leadership

2. Ability to work in a team

3. Communication Skills (written)

4. Problem-solving skills

5. Communication skills (verbal)

6. Strong work ethic

7. Initiative

8. Analytical/quantitative skills

9. Flexibility/adaptability

10. Technical skills

What Do Employers Want to See on Your Resume?

Although professional resume writers would like you to think it's a complex issue that only they can solve for you, this is not necessarily the case. Creating a relevant, informative, and concise resume can be achieved — and it's not rocket science. There are three common things prospective employers are looking for as they quickly scan your resume.

1. They want to know you actually want the job and are qualified for the position.

2. They want to know your strengths, skills, and character.

3. They want to have the details, clearly and accurately stated, so they don't waste time trying to identify these things on your resume.

As important as *what* you say on your resume is *how* you say it. How do you convey to the employer all these things about yourself, and do it in a page or two? Therein lies the challenge. How you create your resume and deliver your relevant information is a major contributor to whether you get the interview. Practicing the three "Cs" is what gets you past this hurdle. Before you submit your resume, make sure it is...

- Complete

- Concise

- Correct

Making Your Resume Complete

In your attempts to make your resume as complete as possible, you walk a fine line between delivering only partial information or that it will be so long that the manager will think they are reading your first novel. For those with little experience, this is not such an issue. However, if you have a ton of experience, how do you know what information to include and what to omit?

Keep asking yourself if what you are including is relevant to the position for which you are applying. For example, if you want to be considered for an accounting position, omit the experiences that do not relate to accounting. That's a no-brainer, but what about if you are applying for a position as an administrative assistant with no previous experience? That's when the type of resume you use becomes paramount in your decision. Since you have no previous administrative assistant jobs to prove your qualifications, you must draw from jobs you have had in the past that have taught you the skills you will need for the position. That's the benefit of using the functional resume.

Now the question is, how can you identify those skills? The first thing you do is review the job posting. Look at the keywords being used. For administrative assistant, you will most likely see words like organized, detail-oriented, team player, good communicator, proficient on the computer, etc. After you have identified these keywords, do a little brainstorming. List each word separately on a sheet of paper. Now, under each word, list the words you would use to describe that skill. Use some of those that were provided earlier in the chapter.

Once you have the descriptive words that you want to use in your resume, think of an instance in one of your previous positions where you can match that word to something you did. Let's say one of your descriptive words to illustrate that you are organized is the word "maintained." Now, begin asking yourself the following questions.

- What did you maintain in another job?

- What was the number of the things you maintained?

- For how many people did you maintain these things?

- How did your maintaining these things make others' jobs easier?

- What was the company or your employer able to decrease or increase because you did such a good job maintaining these things?

- How did you maintain them better than the person who did the job before you?

- What were the results of your maintenance system?

You can ask yourself the same questions with any word, and these questions will help you to form your qualifications and achievement statements. Let's do the same thing with a concrete skill, such as being proficient on the computer.

- What computer skills did you use in another job?

- How did your computer skills make others' jobs easier?

- How did your employer benefit from your computer skills?

- For how many people did you perform these computer skills?

- How was your job made better because of your computer skills?

- What was your company or employer about to increase or decrease based on your computer skills?

- What were the results of having such good computer skills? Were you given a raise, promotion, an award, etc.?

You can see that the brainstorming takes a bit of time, but taking the time now will give you a significant payoff later on — specifically during the interview. Going through all the descriptive words for every skill and qualification you plan to use will give you complete and detailed information. Once you have accumulated all this information, you need to make sure it is delivered in a concise manner.

Making Your Resume Concise

Already on track with making your resume relevant and using keywords, there are also some words to avoid. The following words have been overused, are yesterday's descriptive words, or are too vague.

Words and Phrases Not to Use in Your Resume

- Think outside the box

- Bottom line

- Go-to person

- Very hard worker

- Goal-oriented

- Team player

- Start the ground running

- Self-motivated

- Over-achiever

When employers see these words, they say to themselves—"Oh yeah, you and the other hundred applicants in this pile." These words trigger negative reactions from employers who have seen these words and phrases hundreds of time; they immediately look for proof. Here's the kicker! If you have given them proof, you don't need the word to tell them — show them you are those things. Let your qualifications speak for themselves. Just writing the word is empty and meaningless; anybody can write the phrase "over-achiever." Show them you have been an over-achiever in your other positions, and avoid telling them by just writing the phrase.

Avoid Redundancy and Remove Unnecessary Articles

Don't use the same action verbs when describing your skills and qualifications. It's redundant to say "I'm looking for a job..." Of course you are looking for a job! The employer already knows that because he or she is looking at your resume. Avoid stating the obvious. Remove many of the articles in your sentences, such as "the," "an," and "a;" they can create wordiness in your resume.

Make Every Word Count

Vague statements give little information and take up valuable space on your resume. For example, instead of saying "I assisted with the filing of paperwork," it would be more relevant and precise to say "Maintained personnel files for 150 employees, using the numerical, KolorKode system."

Making Your Resume Correct

To ensure your resume has the best opportunity of getting you the interview, it must be free of typos and grammatical errors. When you have spent hours developing the content, you've looked at it 101 times, it may be difficult for you to see the mistakes. You know what you want it to say, so your mind jumps over the mistakes and continues to make sense of the content. Be diligent about proofing your resume. How embarrassing would it be to have described yourself in your resume as a detail-oriented person and then submit a resume with several glaring mistakes? One mistake can significantly discount all the other things you have said in your descriptions.

Some candidates believe they have done a good job proofing their resume, but they still miss quite a bit. Here are some suggestions to make sure you're submitting a well-written, correct resume.

Ten Steps to Proofing Your Resume

1.   Don't just read through it on your computer screen. Print it out and see what it looks like on paper.

2.   Read your resume aloud. Make yourself pronounce every word. In doing so, you're bound to catch any duplicated words or redundancies.

3.   As you read aloud, slowly follow each word along the line with a pointer pen. This will make your mind stop to consider each word, instead of skipping and scanning.

4.   Read your resume backward. This forces you to stop at each word.

5.   Check for inconsistencies, such as bullet point alignments, punctuation at the end of the bullet

points, capital letters at the beginning of each bullet point, etc. One way to ensure accuracy with your bullet points is to use end punctuation if the bullet point is one or more complete sentences. Leave off end punctuation if it is a single word or phrase.

6. Ask a friend to review your resume for the three "Cs." Make sure they ask themselves the following questions.

- Is the resume complete?

- Is the resume concise?

- Is the resume correct?

7. Pay attention to the titles and headings. Many forget these areas when proofing.

8. If you have copied and pasted, be sure to proof for correct font type and size.

9.   Check to make sure your contact information is correct.

10.   If you have added references to your resume, is their contact information correct? More importantly, have you notified them and asked their permission to use them as a reference?

When you have made the necessary changes, print your resume out one more time to make sure your formatting is consistent and correct. A good practice is also to email and fax your resume to yourself and see what it looks like online. If it does not hold its format, or if your margins are so small that it cuts off the end of lines when faxed, you'll need to correct those issues.

Online submissions create a whole other set of proofing issues, but those will be addressed in a later chapter as we talk about the particular challenges of submitting resumes online.

Chapter 4: The "Black Hole" of Online Resumes

The Internet can be an effective and much more efficient tool when creating resumes, but it has also been referred to as the "Black Hole." Although many managers believe online submissions and screening saves a great deal of time, their reasoning is questionable.

The reality is that it hasn't made the process easier for managers or prospective employees, and here's why. Hundreds, if not thousands, of candidates send blanket submissions to any company for any position they might be remotely interested in or for which they might be slightly qualified. Therefore, managers are expected to sift through all the submissions until they find just a handful of qualified candidates with a genuine desire to work for the company.

In the chaffing process, many suitable candidates are overlooked or don't pass the ATS cut because the online screening does not allow for the human element or that part of the applicant's personality that would make him or her a better fit for the company. The online screening strictly examines the keywords for matches to the hiring manager's stated needs and wants. What is left out could be far more important than a few buzz words the computer is looking to match.

It's no secret that many legitimate candidates who may be lacking a skill here or there, but who are fast learners and responsible workers, have been cast into the "Black Hole" of resumes — never to be reviewed by a hiring manager. They simply get lost in the mountain of submissions.

Most candidates are no strangers to the online abyss, having submitted hundreds of resumes without ever even receiving an acknowledgment. If there is a response from the company, it's evident that it is a computer generated "Dear John — don't call us, we'll call you" response.

The process only gets worse when the employer insists on the candidate first filling out their computer-generated electronic application. Paul Harty, president of Seven Step, says their studies have shown four major issues that job seekers experience when completing online applications.

1. *Not Responsive to Candidates*

Twenty-five percent of the candidates who responded to the survey said they never got a response from the employer after submitting their online application. Seniors seemed to hold the title for being the most likely to be ignored, with approximately 45 percent reporting they never heard from the prospective employer.

2. *Online Applications Take Forever to Complete*

Many of the online applications take 30 to 40 minutes to complete. This limits the number of online submissions you can make in a day— working at it continuously, no more than six or seven. If you believe it's a numbers game, then it could take months to get an interview. If the company requires multiple interviews with associates and upper management, the process can go on until you're ready for retirement!

What's worse is when you get halfway through the application, and you need a timeout for more than 10-15 minutes, many of these online application systems will kick you out, and you'll have to start all over. Or, you think you've finished the process and click submit, only to be sent back to several categories that you have not filled out correctly.

Not only is your time limited, but your response space is also restricted. If you exceed the allotted characters, the computer will not allow you to submit the information. If you cut and paste, and the document extends past the limited number of characters, your information can also be deleted. What started out to be a well-organized and thorough resume can end up being a chopped mess — but it fits the space, right?

3. *Communications Are Limited*

Not only do you get no response from the prospective employer, but you also have no way to follow up with them either. Most of the time, the candidates are not given the name of the hiring manager, so any follow-up becomes a "To Whom It May Concern" endeavor. Many of the positions have already been filled, and the candidates' application falls into the Black Hole, even if their skills and unique talents would have been ideal for another position within the company. There is no resume referral system — just resume fallout.

The way some of the electronic submissions have been designed is that candidates are left to wonder whether or not their resume was actually submitted. No reassuring message verifies their application has been received, and they hear nothing further from the employer. Those candidates who use online submissions as their only form of job seeking can sink into the depressing darkness, believing themselves to be a non-hirable.

4.   *The Inadequate and Unrewarding Automated Response*

One of the ways to get around this lack of response is to look on the company's website and try to contact the hiring manager directly. If it's an upper-management position, you might be able to follow up with your prospective employer. If you are submitting a resume for a higher-income job, you may want to begin the submission process directly, avoiding the online process altogether.

When candidates are offered nothing more than a formal response saying that their resume has been received and is being considered, it can mean different things to different candidates. To the inexperienced newbies, it means "Oh boy, I'm being considered for the job!" While experienced candidates who have received the exact response from dozens of employers, say to themselves, "Another one bites the dust." You just cannot help but wonder how the employer would feel if the shoe were on the other foot. And yet, employers report that they are desperate for qualified candidates.

Why is it there are so many highly skilled and talented people looking for a job and so many employers who say they cannot find qualified candidates? Could it be the inadequate screening process that many of these companies are using? Absolutely! Peter Cappelli, a management professor at The Wharton School of the University of Pennsylvania, reported recently that there was a company's screening system that had received 29,000 applicants' resumes for an engineering position and found none to be qualified for the job.

Now, what do you think the odds were that not one in 29,000 applicants were not qualified? Could it be that the screening system was looking for the perfect candidate? Unfortunately, there is no perfect candidate — only the best in the pile from which you choose. Some candidates who are innovative and creative might have shown that on their resume — but, they were discarded. Others might have been qualified, but their format was a little off — out the door without so much as a thank you from the computer. Companies want people who are inventive, but they create such a small box to place qualified applicants, that the creative sorts fall by the wayside.

It's a complex problem that today's candidates must address. Applicants must first please the computer to get permission to speak to the hiring manager. The computer has become the gatekeeper of resumes; what candidates need to do is find the key that opens the gate to get the interview. Whether you're for online submissions or not, today's job market requires you include it as a resource for your searches. Based on a study by Pew Research Center, 79 percent of Americans who have looked for a job in the last two years have utilized online submissions, and 34 percent report it as being one of the most valuable tools available to them in their search for available jobs.

The formatting for online resumes is much different from those that are mailed or handed directly to the prospective employer. You just have a whole other set of problems when submitting an online resume. It can be quite challenging for candidates to keep current with today's online demands, but to be successful in your job search, it's crucial to learn a few things that can mean the difference between falling into the "Black Hole" or getting an interview.

The Difference Between a Human Reader and a Computer Reader

There is a huge difference between how a human reads a resume and how a computer reads it. Helping a person quickly review your resume and find it aesthetically pleasing, candidates need to pay attention to parallel formatting, consistent fonts, and clear, attractive, and easy-to-read organization. Humans look for active verbiage that captures and holds their interest, and detailed descriptions of qualifications and skills. They look for powerful leaders and cooperative team players and determine the candidates' soft skills by the descriptive words they use. Because humans can distinguish and think about what isn't said as well as what is revealed in the resume, they can read between the lines.

Computers have a straight-up, take-you-for-your-word, type of approach. Computers don't care about the aesthetic or eye-candy appeal of your resume; they are just searching your resume for words and phrases to make matches to the manager's stated needs and wants. It's not making value judgments, or impressed by a skill you have that was not previously asked for on the job posting. No! The computer is unemotionally performing the task it was asked to do. In fact, some computers get confused by any fancy graphics or resume formatting, including bullet points, bolded and underlined text, and italics.

To make sure your resume isn't tripping up the computer's ability to correctly process your submission, create a "text-only" version. Text-only resumes are universal to all computer systems and platforms. Text-only resumes are also called ASCII versions. If you are faxing or emailing your resume, an ASCII version can be easily scanned and put into the employer's screening system. Some managers prefer to receive your resume in a text-only format. Let's examine the steps of how to create an ASCII version of your resume.

Creating an ASCII Version of Your Resume

These are general instructions, but they might vary depending on the software you are using.

1. Use your word processing program and go up to "file" in your menu bar. Then move your cursor to "save as" and click on "text only" or "ASCII." Title your document something easy for you to remember, such as "Internet resume."

2. Now, close your word processing program, and open the file in your "ASCII" version. Notice that the resume no longer has any formatting.

3. Because the "text only" version has no formatting, you will need to go through it and make some changes. Reviewing it line by line, making sure all text is flush to the left margin.

4. Change all the text that is "centered," or justified to the left or right margins.

5.   You shouldn't be able to see any graphics or artwork, but you might see some special character formatting like bullet points or asterisks. Remove all of them.

6.   Omit all the tabbed characters.

7.   Take out all the columns.

8.   If you feel it's necessary, you can replace the bulleted points with an ASCII asterisk (*).

9.   Lastly, go back through and re-proof your resume. Make sure you haven't omitted necessary text.

10.   You can use ASCII keyboard characters to enhance the visual appearance of your resume.

When you have created an ASCII version of your resume, it will be readable on any computer system, and you can easily upload it to online automated application sites. As many downsides as there are to online submissions, think of all the many benefits the Internet has provided for candidates. Once you have computer proofed your resume, you can apply, with little to no out-of-pocket-cost, to many prospective employers all over the country—the world, for that matter.

At this day and age, you cannot afford to be computer illiterate. If the thought of submitting your resume online turns your legs to jelly, it's time for you to suck it up and bite the bullet. The computer can be an amazing resource, and leaving it out of your portfolio of useful tools is a big mistake. Doing so could cost you the job of your dreams.

Offer to take one of your computer whiz friends out to dinner in exchange for some help with your online submissions. Realize, though, there will be a learning curve, so be patient with yourself; it's bound to take you a little longer at first, and you might run into some snags along the way. Once you get through a few submissions of your resumes online, you'll get more familiar with the process, and it won't be so daunting.

Timing Is Everything

Another factor to keep in mind when submitting your resume is determining when — when is the best time and day to send your resume? Studies have shown that the best time and day to send your resume is early Monday morning. It's the beginning of the week, and there are most likely few resumes lined up before yours. On Mondays, the manager's minds are fresh, and they are more likely to be patient enough to give your resume more than a 10-second read. If you are submitting your resume online, be the first one of the day.

If you are emailing or faxing your resume to human resources or a recruiter, it's a good idea not to do so on Friday afternoons. Everybody's minds are on the weekend, and they are already one foot out the door. Your resume is much more likely to be overlooked when sent on a Friday afternoon. Most candidates are unconcerned about timing, but you don't want to be like most candidates. It's time for you to stand out in the crowd, don't you think?

Clean Up Your Social Media Sites

As much as you want employers to review your online resumes, there might be things on your social media sites you don't want them to see. Clean those things up before submitting your resumes. Then, be sure to give your prospective employer access to your Facebook, Twitter, and LinkedIn accounts. First of all, be certain you have created these sites and that they represent you in a professional, friendly manner. You would be amazed how many employers have refused to hire a qualified candidate because of what they read on their social media. Facebook is one of the most popular social media accounts that employers review. It is there that people reveal their true selves — sometimes way too much of their true selves.

Keep in mind; Facebook isn't like Las Vegas. What is written on Facebook stays on Facebook, and it is there for anyone to see — even your employers. It is incredible how many people don't have a "private" life anymore. They post everything on Facebook. While this can be entertaining for you and your friends, your candor can be disheartening for employers to view. They have pictured you as being a professional; suddenly they see you posting pictures of you and your friends that may not represent you in the best light. Not only is this poor judgment, but it can cost you a lot of heartaches throughout the years.

So, before posting your resumes online, go through your photos and remove those that could be offensive. Put them on a disc and save them for another place, another time. Remove comments that put you in a bad light. Look at your friends and their posted comments. Also, pay attention to what you have posted on your friends' sites. You can bet that a savvy employer is also looking at the company you keep.

Keeping several versions of your resume on your computer is recommended. One that is a .pdf format, one that is "text-only" or "ASCII," and one that you will take with you to hand to your future employer. Since you will be sending out different resumes and different versions of your resumes, it's a good idea to track this information, so you know what you have sent to whom. There's no time like the present to start creating a fantastic resume, and one that is easily read online as well.

Chapter 5: Ten Tips for Resume Excellence

Once you have created the first draft of your resume, it's time to go back and turn it into an attention getter. The question is — HOW? How do you change a resume from average to excellent? Here are ten tips to help you achieve resume excellence.

Tip #1: *Make sure you have included all your contact information.*

Of course, you have provided the prospective employer with the regular stuff, such as your name, address, phone numbers, etc. At the risk of sounding like a midnight infomercial, "But wait — there's more!" Did you forget to include your email address? A word of caution — make sure you use an email address that isn't cutesy. Employers won't consider you a professional if you're using an email like catsrule@gmail.com, or harrybarry@aol.com. If your email sounds silly, get one that doesn't to be used on your resume.

Also, don't forget to include a link to your social media accounts on your resume. Remember, do some cleanup on your sites if necessary — before you submit your resume. Don't give the employer an excuse not to interview you. Keep it professional. You also might want to include a brief video of achievements and post them on LinkedIn or Twitter, and make sure it shows personality as well as your professionalism. If you give the hiring manager links to your social media sites, make it worthwhile for them to visit your page. Because your social media sites are more visual, a manager who's interested enough in you to visit your site will usually spend more time there than with your resume. Get them hooked by your visual presentation.

Tip #2: Don't include a photo or video with your resume.

Some candidates think they must do something outside the norm to be considered creative and establish a new standard of excellence. Most employers will tell you that what's outside the norm is clear, concise, and relevant resumes. They normally don't get to read many resumes like that. Although you would think those types are typical and traditional — this isn't normally the case, as nice as it may be. Traditional can be a good thing when creating a resume. Your employer will know where to quickly look on your resume to find the information they need.

Photos, graphs, and videos will do more harm than good when turned in along with your resume, especially when trying to pass the ATS screening. If you want to add those things after, and it's not essential that you do, you can do so when invited for the interview. The more fluff you add to your resume, the more reasons you give the employer not to hire you. Keep your resume concise yet descriptive. A photo or video of yourself is just more fluff, so omit it. You can be sure that managers are not going to take the time to play your video while they're going through hundreds of other candidates.

One of the things you may want to include when you get the interview is a video business card. They are a bit pricey, so be conservative when you share them. They are still different enough to be intriguing and capture the interest of your prospective employer, so they are more likely to play the brief video card.

Tip #3: *Make sure your cellphone message is professional.*

If one of your contact numbers is your cell phone, be sure to make your voicemail message professional. It should be something more than just "Leave a message," and it should not be a celebrity's voice singing your message, or your child telling them mommy can't come to the phone right now because she's changing baby brother's diaper. It doesn't have to be flashy of entertaining, and it doesn't have to be a commercial about all your skills and talents. Few people enjoy commercials on television, much less being made to sit through one when trying to schedule an interview.

What can be heard in the background of your message can also be quite annoying, so call yourself and make sure there isn't a dog barking or a baby crying as your voicemail plays. You may have grown so accustomed to your everyday sounds that these things escape your attention. However, when you play them back, you'll realize you may need a few more recording attempts. Keep in mind; your employers are busy, so your message should not be too long. Be respectful of their time constraints.

Tip #4: Create a captivating summary at the beginning of the resume.

Jane Heifetz, the principal of Right Resumes, LLC and contributing editor for Harvard Business Review says, "It's a rich, accomplishment-focused summary that will stop the reader in her tracks and keep her from passing you over for the next candidate." If hiring managers only give your resume a 20-second glance, they might only be reading your summary before jumping to the next resume. Make every word in your summary count.

A "standout" summary should contain the following information.

- Begin with a brief phrase or sentence that describes your profession.

- Follow that phrase with an achievement that makes you stand out from the average candidate. What will make the hiring manager sit up and pay closer attention when they review your summary?

- Then, end the summary with two or three additional statements, which should include information such as:

- A specific, well-phrased accomplishment

- An award or promotion that resulted from your stated achievement

- A mix of skills that will be of benefit to your hiring manager based on what was included in the available posted position

- One or two personal characteristics that are relevant to the position

- Specific numbers or percentages that prove your value to the company

The following are some examples of well-written, concise, intriguing summaries that speak to the employer's needs and wants in an employee.

Over 20 years as a creative writer/program developer with a track record of producing extraordinary results for more than 50 national and community-based corporations. A commitment to learning and an enthusiastic innovator with excellent technical, research, and organizational skills.

Fifteen years' worth of sales training experience with ten of the country's top new home builders, inspiring individual and team development that resulted in less turnover and more sales. Created positive sales environment through the recognition and development of individual potential that contributes to establishing a balanced, productive team environment.

Tip #5: Include awards and personal achievements on your resume.

If the awards and accomplishments are relevant to the position for which you are applying, incorporate them into your resume — notice the word "relevant." If you were first runner-up in a beauty pageant, the chances are that's not going to be of interest unless you are applying for a pageant coach and it's important that you know how to create a winner. Besides being relevant, make your awards and achievements specific. Stating the what, where, and when gives your awards punch and your statements power.

For example, if you were given an award for performance, structure it so that your employer will see the value in the award. If you were a contributing writer for a magazine, perhaps your award would sound something like this.

Received the 2016 "National Publisher of the Year" award for opening the largest magazine first edition in company history, resulting in over $500,000 in ad revenue over a period of six months.

Tip #6: Include relevant volunteer work in your resume.

By relevant, that doesn't mean that you volunteered in the same organization or even the same field or industry. What is relevant are the skills you used or gained from the experience, especially the soft skills. This is the opportunity for you to display your character and personality. For instance, if you volunteered with the Rotary club to act as a liaison between school clubs and community leaders, take those communication and leadership skills and make them relevant to the position for which you are applying.

Tip #7: List professional affiliations/military experience on your resume.

Even if you must create a two-page resume because you listed your military experience and professional affiliations, it's a good idea to do so. These experiences are usually rich in translatable skills and achievements, and many managers can personally relate to both. Everybody likes others who give of themselves, to the community and their country, so don't be shy about putting them on your resume. You have earned the right to include such experiences, and they reveal your responsibility, reliability, and character.

Tip #8: Let Your Achievements S.O.A.R. in your resume.

It's not enough to describe your achievements in vague terms; you need to write them in such a way that they S.O.A.R. Showing you a "before" and "after" statement will illustrate what is meant by S.O.A.R.

Before Statement

Managed a large crew of workers.

Now apply the S.O.A.R. method of writing your achievements.

S = Statement that shows action — be specific!

O = Occurrence of that action — how often?

A = Amount of action — how much or how many?

R = Result of the action — what was the outcome of your efforts?

After applying the S.O.A.R., here's what your achievement statement reads like.

Managed a 20-man crew of sanitation workers on a daily basis, and increased safety measures by 20% over a 12-month period while decreasing the cost of heavy-equipment repair by $43,000. Created greater job satisfaction through a company recognition program that celebrated sanitation workers' value to the company by including monthly contributions in the company newsletter and organizing an annual company picnic.

Tip #9: Show evidence that you enjoy learning on your resume.

Almost every hiring manager knows you are not going to have all the skills required for the job posting, so don't feel you need to embellish. What *is* helpful is to show the employer you enjoy learning and welcome ongoing job training to improve your skills. This is done by showing different training you have participated in on previous jobs. Make sure you explain in detail using the S.O.A.R. method of writing. Don't just say that you attended an Excel class. Instead, write something like this.

"Attended an advanced Excel class that resulted in more complete and informative weekly reports that created more opportunities for salespeople to bid on 10 percent more construction jobs over a 12-month period."

Tip #10: Make your best stand out from the rest.

Keep in mind that hiring managers give your resumes a cursory glance and then make a quick decision to include you in their "for more consideration" pile.

Because this is how the game is played, you need to make sure you place your best within the top half of your resume. Give your best more room on the page, but don't make it a bigger, bolder font to stand out from your other information. Keep it clean and uniform.

What makes your resume stand out is the time you spend on each one submitted to ensure it is tailor made for that one job posting. What will also make your resume outstanding is to understand the following two things.

1.   Make sure that you are qualified for the job. It's important that you have at least 75-80 percent of the required skills, and that you can prove that by your achievement descriptions. If you decide to send your resume in for a job that interests you, but one in which you are borderline on the skills needed, then you'll need to show the prospective employer that you are enthusiastic and a quick study. If there are a few skills you lack, show them you are willing to put in the time to learn them. Don't apologize for your lack of competencies. In fact, don't tell them you don't have the skills.

Remember, your resume is about showing them — so, show them you are smart and ambitious, and you have learned new tasks well in the past.

2. The second way to make sure your resume is outstanding is only to send in your resume to jobs you want — to jobs that you can feel excited about the possibilities of getting an interview. If you don't care about the job, or if the job is just a stop gap for you, then that is going to show in your resume. If not in the resume, it will appear in the interview. You will have wasted your time and that of the hiring manager.

When you want the job, it's good to voice it. If you get a chance to interview for the position, don't be shy about telling the employer how excited you are about meeting them. Thank them for giving you the interview. Excitement and enthusiasm go a long way in making your meeting memorable.

It never fails: apply for a job that you don't care that much about getting, and the next thing you know you're being given an invitation to interview. Some think it's just Murphy's Law—what you don't want, you get, right? However, it could be something entirely different. It could be that you are more relaxed when the stakes aren't quite so high. It's tough to be calm and casual when you want the job so badly you can taste it.

What helps is when you have several pans in the fire— some promising resumes out there, so you don't feel like the sky is falling if you bomb out on one. There will be another one to take its place. When you are diligently looking for a job, you can't afford to submit a resume and then wait to get a response before sending in another. Flood the market with resumes; just make sure each one is tailor made for each position. Don't flood the market with the same resume and a "To Whom It May Concern" cover letter.

When possible, get the names of the hiring manager and address your cover letter to that person. You may have to make a phone call to the human resources department. It's legitimate to tell them you'd like to personalize your cover letter and need the name of the hiring manager. The worse that could happen is they say no, and then what have you lost?

What often holds candidates back from creating outstanding resumes and thoughtful submissions is they lack boldness and enthusiasm. If you've been at this job seeking game for quite some time, you can get stale, and your attitude becomes one of sarcasm and disdain. Guard against that; if you let those negative feelings take over, they will bleed through to your resume and personal interviews. Stay up — stay fresh — and anticipate the best!

Chapter 6: 20 Items to Remove from Your Resume

Not all resume writers agree on what to include and what to remove, but this is a thorough list of what you might want to consider taking out of your resume.

1.   *Salary History*

No good can come of including a salary history. Telling your next employer what your last employer was willing to pay and you were prepared to accept can only limit the salary offered or put you out of the salary range planned for this position. If the employer should ask you for a salary history, give them a broad range, with the low end being slightly higher than you are willing to take and the high end being slightly lower than you would love to be paid.

2.   *Jobs from more than 10 years ago*

If you've been on one job for more than ten years, you might want to include one more beyond the 10-year limit. Otherwise, omit all the jobs you've had older than ten years. If you are creating a functional resume, use the skills you have learned over the years, but don't include all the jobs.

3. *Expected Skills*

Avoid including skills that every candidate is expected to have, such as Microsoft Word and general computer skills.

4. *Short-Term Jobs*

Even if it's been within the 10-year timeframe, avoid including short-term jobs. Too many jobs during that period will make it look as though you've been job hopping.

5. *A Bio*

Prospective employers don't want to know about you; they want to know what you can do for them — how hiring you will make them the hero.

6. Acronyms

Our society seems to revolve around acronyms these days. Avoid using them, even if you are certain the employer should know what they mean. Because even if they know what the acronym means, seeing more acronyms than words can be quite annoying. And, the ATS screening software may not understand the acronym.

7. Cliché and Adages

If a phrase has been around long enough to be considered a cliché, then it's too tired and dull to be included in a resume. Also, using old adages can make your resume sound preachy. There is no room to include information that isn't necessary and relevant.

8. Controversial Interests or Hobbies

If you enjoy competing in dangerous sports or take pride in your scorpion collection, the company may see these things as reasons for you to lose work time. Keep your unusual hobbies and interests off your resume and social media sites.

9. *Political or Religious Beliefs*

Your beliefs and values might give your employer a reason not to call you in for an interview. Give them a chance to get to know you before you begin philosophical discussions that invite heated debates.

10. *Long Descriptive Paragraphs*

There is no space to waste on a 1-2 page resume. The information is easier read when bulleted instead of writing long, drawn out paragraphs.

11. *Orphan Words*

One word lines are a waste of real estate on a resume. Make your sentence more concise and avoid the orphans.

12.   *Your Address*

Some say you shouldn't include your full address — just your city and state. The reasoning behind this belief is that if your employer considers you too far from the workplace, they might think you'll soon be looking for a job closer to home. Some employers also worry about long-distance employees having a habit and excuse for being repeatedly late.

13.   *Current Work Email Address*

This should be a no-brainer, but it's surprising how many employers say that they viewed current employees' emails and saw requests for interviews from other employers. Also, new employers might think, if you would do it to your current employer, you'll do it to them. Avoid the issues altogether, and use a private email address.

14.   *The Overuse of Bullet Points*

The accepted number of bullet points under each category is no more than six. If you're on your tenth bullet point, you need to make your thoughts and items more concise or do a better job of prioritizing and end the list at six bullet points.

15.   *Things Relating to High School*

When showing your education, begin with college degrees or courses. Anything from high school is unnecessary and, most likely, irrelevant.

16.   *Big Words*

If you're using big words to make you sound intelligent, they're probably not going to do the trick. What will make you appear knowledgeable are your skills and qualifications — not the length of your words.

17. *Industry Jargon*

Even though the hiring manager might know what the term means, if your resume is being reviewed by a recruiter or a human resources person, it may be vague and confusing for them. Avoid using this type of language.

18. *Vague Words*

Don't say "sometimes," give the reader a time frame or frequency of occurrence. Instead of saying "sort of" or "pretty sure," be specific. Use pointed language that qualifies your statements.

19. *Negative Words*

Avoid using words with a negative connotation, even if you are using them in a positive way. For example, instead of saying "aggressive," you might want to substitute the word "assertive." Instead of using the word "demanded," you might use "delegated."

Words with negative connotations leave a negative residue in the minds of employers. You want them to be thinking positive thoughts of you before and during the interview.

20. *Omit All the Typos*

There should be no typos, spelling errors, repeated words, grammatical mistakes, or punctuation inconsistencies on your resume.

The biggest issue that you want to omit on your resume is anything that is not true. Even more than embellishing your skills, telling outright lies on your resume will only be discovered later when you cannot perform or don't have the background knowledge needed to do the required task.

Don't name drop notable people's names if you don't know the person or have never interned under them, or cannot substantiate the information about your important person. In fact, too much name dropping can make you appear to be what is known as a "topper," and few people can relate or even like toppers. Toppers are people who always "one up" whatever you say or do. If you've climbed Mount Everest, they've climbed Mount Everest with one arm tied behind their back. Name dropping begins to be a game of "anything you can do, I can do better."

Trying to be someone you're not only causes you embarrassment and your prospective employer annoyance. Being yourself is always the best policy, and besides, it's too difficult to keep up the pretense that lying on a resume can cause. It's incredible how many people have lied on their resumes, but most get caught down the road and suffer public shame. Save yourself the worry and anxiety of wondering when the ax will fall. If you get the position based on a lie, you'll usually end up losing it under similar circumstances — like being fired for not being trustworthy, or being demoted for lack of skills or knowledge.

Focus on the best you have to offer, and be willing to work on improving or developing your weaknesses. Giving it your best is all your prospective employer can expect. Hard work, honesty, and determination are some of the best traits and skills any employee can possess.

Conclusion: Effective Follow Up

You've created a tailor-made resume, submitted it, and now it's been a while, and you've heard nothing. How do you know what and when to follow up? When does good follow up become desperate pestering? A few things to keep you busy while you're waiting — create and submit more tailored resumes. Don't stop and wait; it will drive you crazy. Keep on working hard to find exciting opportunities that you are qualified for, and then start the process all over again. That way, you're not putting so much importance on one position where you are tempted to make a pest of yourself with too much follow up.

Don't follow up with a random call or email to somebody — anybody — in human resources. Try to find out the name of the hiring manager so that you can follow up on a more personal note. It may take a few phone calls before you discover the hiring manager's name, so be persistent. Once you determine who the hiring manager is, decide whether you want to follow up by phone or email. There's a fine line between showing interest and enthusiasm for the position and going over-board with your contacts. If you're in question, it's better to err on the side of too little than too much follow up.

Review the job posting again to see if it contains a submission close date. Some don't, but if it does, it is typical to wait a week after the end date to make a follow-up contact. If there is no close date, wait at least a week after you have submitted your resume. Whether you follow up by phone or email, here are a few suggested questions to ask.

- I sent in my resume last week and was wondering if you could tell me — has the decision been made for the accounting position yet?

- When do you expect to be making your decision?

- Would it be alright if I got back in touch with you next week?

- How would you prefer to be contacted?

Always thank whoever answers the phone for taking the time to speak with you about the job. If you call and leave a message, don't place another call for a while; one voicemail is sufficient. Calling two or three times a week is bordering on the pestering side. If you decide to call for your follow-up contact, make sure the job posting doesn't instruct candidates not to call.

In most situations, it's a good idea not to be too familiar or casual when you follow up. Don't say, "Remember me!?" Of course they don't remember you; they don't even know you, and most likely couldn't tell you the names of a handful of people who sent in their resumes. Just to be clear, let's review some of the things you don't want to do in your follow up.

Things Not to Do When You Follow Up

- Don't question the hiring manager, such as asking them why they didn't get in touch with you.

- Don't apologize for following up. It's good practice, so there's no need to apologize.

- It can be very frustrating when prospective employers do not respond to your resume but try not to let your frustration be apparent in your voice or a printed email. Always, always be polite, positive, and enthusiastic.

- If this is your second follow-up attempt, resist the temptation to show your anger or ask them why they never got back to you.

- Stay as professional with your follow up as you were with your resume. Just caring enough to follow up will get the attention of your employer; it's not necessary to send a cookie gram or an edible arrangement. If they don't respond, then press on to the next position and send another resume. Wait a while, and then try another follow-up. If you called for the first follow up, make this attempt an email.

- If possible, you might decide to follow up in person. Although it is probable that you won't get a face-to-face meeting with the hiring manager, this is a good time to leave a video business card. Be sure to let the administrator know that it is a video card, and then give them a hand-written note along with the card. The note could say something like this.

Just wanted to come by and introduce myself. Sorry I missed you. Since I didn't get a chance to meet you in person, I'm leaving you my video business card. I'll look forward to hearing from you soon.

Keep it friendly, yet professional. Write the note ahead of time, so it's neat and has no mistakes. If you get to speak with the hiring manager in person, just tuck the card away.

- If there has been something positive in the news about the company or your prospective employer, refer to it in your note. If the news is not so positive, leave it alone. For example, if the company just went public, you might congratulate them on their success in going public. This will let the hiring manager know that you are interested enough to keep track of their success and want to be a contributing member. Be sure to sign the personalized note, and put an email and phone number below your signature.

- If you accept a job with another company, send notes to those you have applied with and ask to be removed from consideration for the position, explaining that you have accepted employment with another company. This will leave you in good standing, should you want to contact them in the future.

- Don't send your prospective employer a thank you card if you haven't had any response from them. Obviously, there's nothing to thank them for, and the card might be taken as a form of sarcasm.

- One candidate followed up with this: *"I am considering taking a position with your rival, but since you were my first choice I wanted to try one more time to get in touch with you."* It's a bold move, but it does show confidence and enthusiasm for the job.

If you haven't heard from the company, and you figure you've got nothing to lose, you may want to try something bold like the last candidate mentioned. Just know that it could be perceived as a bit pushy.

As you work through the process of creating and submitting your resume, the best thing to do is experiment a bit to see what works best for you. Push yourself to keep moving forward. If you feel yourself getting down because there's little activity, change things up a bit. Try a different job board, or go to some companies in person to give them your resume. Apply directly on the company's website. See if any of your friends have contacts with a company you might be interested in applying at, and ask them to keep you in mind the next time there is an opening for which you might be qualified.

Set daily and weekly goals of how many resumes you are going to submit that day and that week. Then, set follow-up goals for yourself as well. Make the goals attainable, but push yourself. Don't settle for turning in just a few resumes a week and then pulling your hair out as you wait for a response. The best remedy for discouragement is to stay busy, keep trying, and refuse to give a voice to any negative thoughts.

In any job market, it can take a while to find your dream job, and there's only so much time you can sit at your computer to create and submit resumes. Volunteer someplace where you might like to work, while you're waiting for a response to your submissions. Many people have gained full-time employment from a job where they began as a volunteer.

You can also do some company research, preparing for an interview should you be invited for one. Prepare some questions that you'd like to ask, and you'll have something to say when they ask you if you have any questions. If you get really desperate, clean out your kitchen junk drawer, change the oil in your car, prepare a gourmet meal for your working spouse — anything to stay occupied and keep you from getting frustrated or depressed.

Most of all, stay focused on continuing your job search, and on dedicating yourself to getting your dream job. Trying to find a job can be a full-time job in and of itself. In the job seeking process, you'll learn things that will help you when you are someday in a hiring position. Remember what it was like for you, and don't do to other candidates what might have been done to you. Be courteous and polite, understand their challenges, and try to be fair in the hiring process.

Meanwhile, good luck in your efforts to find the job you've always dreamed of having — and put your best resume forward.

Thanks for making it through to the end of *Resume: The Definitive Guide on Writing a Professional Resume to Land You Your Dream Job*. I hope that it was informative and able to provide you with all of the tools you need to achieve your goals, whatever they may be.

The next step is to start creating winning resumes that help open the doors to great career opportunities.

Finally, if you found this book useful in anyway, a review on Amazon is always appreciated!

Good luck in your professional endeavors,

David Barron

About the Author

David Barron is a performance coach and management consultant from Vancouver, Canada. Through his work, David aims to guide individuals and executives in reaching their personal and professional goals. His personal mission is to live his life better than he did yesterday, and his goal is to make that mission a reality for every other person that he comes in contact with.

41807661R00066

Made in the USA
Middletown, DE
23 March 2017